Other Books by Loralyn Reynolds

A Whisper of Hope
Animals of the Ark
Along the Banks of the Wyaloosing

FOUR LITTLE FACES

A Story from the Great Depression

A story that happened, told by Nora Detamore to her daughter,
Loralyn and as Cecil Detamore (Aunt Pete) remembered.
With a few little flourishes from Loralyn to add some spice.

Loralyn Reynolds

FOUR LITTLE FACES
A STORY FROM THE GREAT DEPRESSION

iUniverse books may be ordered through booksellers or by contacting:

iUniverse
1663 Liberty Drive
Bloomington, IN 47403
www.iuniverse.com
1-800-Authors (1-800-288-4677)

Because of the dynamic nature of the Internet, any web addresses or links contained in this book may have changed since publication and may no longer be valid. The views expressed in this work are solely those of the author and do not necessarily reflect the views of the publisher, and the publisher hereby disclaims any responsibility for them.

Any people depicted in stock imagery provided by Thinkstock are models, and such images are being used for illustrative purposes only. Certain stock imagery © Thinkstock.

ISBN: 978-1-5320-3865-5 (sc)
ISBN: 978-1-5320-3866-2 (e)

Print information available on the last page.

iUniverse rev. date: 01/04/2018

Dedication

This book/story is dedicated to the Detamore Family, a family huge, noisy, and loving whose care and support I am so grateful for. And especially to the Detamore who gave me birth and linked me with this family, my beloved mother, Nora Elizabeth Detamore Reynolds Westover Neal Ernstes. (1927-2015)

Family Connections, and Introduction

In the 1840s, Clark Highley and his wife, Telitha Wright, of Virginia brought land along the Miami/Grant County line in Indiana, near the town that would become Converse. He farmed there and raised his family. So did his sons. One of those sons, Leroy Highley, who was a Civil war Veteran, married Ida Culp (second wife), and their first born daughter, Madge Bell Highley, married Percy Odwick Detamore (who was her second husband). Their four children are the "Four little Faces". Percy, better known as "Mick", was the third son and fifth child of Deloss Detamore and Nora Rust. He had, at the time of this story, nine living siblings. His older sister, Cecil, better known as "Pete", mothered the family, who had lost their mother in 1915. This story takes place during the Great Depression, (1929-1930s).

The Detamores had become tenant farmers and laborers, but their history was also tied up with the area that the Highleys occupied. Some of Mick's siblings had been born in or near Converse, the little town that straddles the Miami/Grant County lines and is a stone throw away from Howard County, where Mick was born. It was Mick's great grandfather, William Detamore, of Virginia/Ohio who had come to Indiana in the 1800s.

Since the 1840s there has been a Highley or a Highley descendent living in the area. It is so with the Detamores. The Converse cemetery houses ancestors on both sides.

The four Little Faces are the author's mother and her siblings. This story or stories were told to me by my mother and some of it as told to her by her aunt, Aunt 'Pete'. Some of the stories are as my grandfather told them and my Uncle 'Rags' also contributed. The siblings are William 'Bill' Allen Detamore, Wendell 'Lefty' Odwick Detamore, Nora Elizabeth Detamore, and Phillip 'Rags' Warren Detamore. Their half brother was Highley Coan and their half sisters were Lillian, Mary Ann and Martha Coan. Their uncles and aunts include the Detamore group, Forrest 'Fats', Volney 'Bud', Cecil 'Pete', Tressie, Ivan, Mary, Mayora 'Donie', Owen Leroy 'Roy', Fern, and Robert 'Bob'. The Highley group were Anna, Lula, Clove, Harriet, Ted, McKinley and Edna.

In This Life

In this life; I've loved deeply
At times.
I've played hard
At times.
And worked hard,
At times.
I've prayed hard
And wept bitter tears
At times, In this life!

I've dreamed dreams
And seen most come true;
But there was one
Withheld from me;
I don't know why.

So I'll sing in the morning
And laugh at noon
And pray in the evening
To keep my heart in tune;
And I will remember
Not all dreams come true.
But I will make the best
Of what life I have left.
And be grateful
That one broken dream
Didn't keep me from fulfilling
What He had in mind
For me to do.

So eat the bread
And drink the wine
It is God Divine
Gracious and kind,
Who meets us
In the taking of the bread
And the drinking of the wine.
Who in His time
Reveals His purpose
For our lives.

Acknowledgements

I acknowledge the help of Debbie Ruth at the Marion Library and my cousin, Billie, who looked through library files and came up with the most usable on The Orphans Home and the Malleable. And a big thank you to all the Detamores who shared their stories, feelings and impressions of family and life throughout the years.

And a big 'thank you' to the website that gave me information on Converse, and Marion and the Malleable.

Contents

God's Promise to Us

I will be with you for a thousand years
I will be with you through your tears
I will be with you as you combat your fears
I will be with you when the path veers
I will be with you when time stands still
Are you listening? Do you hear?

Converse

If you ask the man on the street, "What do you think of when I say the word, 'Converse'? That man or woman will probably say 'Converse shoes'. Converse shoes have been around for nearly 50 years. In today's world, you can buy a pair for $9.99 up to $250.00.

However my answer would be this. "Converse is the little Indiana town my Uncle Rags was born in and where my grandfather kidnapped his children during the Great Depression. It is also the town where many ancestors are buried."

It is also one of those towns that straddles two counties. Part of the town is in Miami County and the other part is in Grant County. From its inception in 1849, it grew to have a population of over a thousand people. In its heyday, it was an important railroad town. However, it has never had more than 1500 people and today has a population of 1,115 people (2010 census). It is mainly a town that survives because some people like little towns, like my cousin who lives there now and is the daughter of one of the other little faces.

I visited last two years ago. It is a sleepy looking little town. State Highway 18 runs through the town on to Marion. Marion is the largest town in Grant County and where the Four Little Faces were raised, in a section of the city called 'Bucktown'.

By God's Grace

By God's great grace
Those four little faces
Look upon God's faces.
Someone prayed.

The Four Little Faces

Pete paused, frowned and wiped her hands on her apron. She had heard Mick's old truck. She knew the sound of it. It had stopped and, a few minutes later, drove on. That was odd. Why had he not come in? She peered out the front window in time to see the truck moving slowly down the street in the gathering dusk. Then she heard sounds on the porch and then some snuffling. Her thought was, "the dogs are in my flowers again." She flung open the door and looked down. Four little eyes looked up at her. Despair swept through her. What was she going to do?

Everyone was poor then, hit by the depression of the 30s. As later written, it was the darkest of times, following the 1929 stock market crash. People were out of work, families split apart. Even those with work struggled. It was pretty common at that time for a family like the Detamores, Pete's birth family, that whoever had a house was invaded by family members who had recently had to move from theirs. But those two little faces peering up at Pete had their own story, not to mention two more faces that Mick had dropped off at Mary's house. Mary was another sister who lived nearby.

But now was not the time for stories or despair, so Pete pushed hers aside. She would figure out later how to make ends meet. She reached down and swept Nora and Phillip into her arms and gently chided, "Hush, it will be all right. Let us wash your faces and have something to eat. You can sleep with Lenora tonight."

As she wiped noses, she called, "Lenora," and her eleven year old daughter came running into the room, took one glance, and took over the hand and face washing and the comforting. They had been through this before, and she would always be the big sister, not the cousin she really was. Some children need aunts who are mothers and cousins who are sisters, and the four little faces were four such children.

Yes, they had been through this before, Pete pondered, as she finished supper for her family, her two unexpected guests, and her boarders. But always before, she and Mick had sat down and talked about it. She was the oldest sister in the Detamore family. Altogether there had been fourteen siblings, eleven living to adulthood. Mick was four years younger than she and they had always been close, even more so after the death of their beloved mother at 42, leaving the family an infant brother to raise.

Pete's mind continued to wander as she piled the table high with food and the children's voices blended with the greetings from her younger brothers, Roy and Bob, who also lived with her and worked at the Malleable across the street. Well, it was time to set aside her thoughts and get through supper and baths. There would be time for thinking things through when all were in bed and she had some moments to herself.

The Snatching

Finally, the house was quiet except for a snore from one of the men. Pete finished her chores for the evening which included some preparation for breakfast the next morning. Now she could sit a few minutes and contemplate the series of events that had brought them to this place. She sank gratefully into a favorite rocking chair and closed her eyes and let the memories flow. She loved her nephews and her niece. They indeed seemed like her own, but they were Mick's children, and his responsibility. She had tried so hard to talk him out of his marriage to Madge Highley Coan, but he was young and determined. Madge was odd, too odd, and Pete had always been wary of her. She was also a divorcee with four children by her first marriage. What man needed to take on a ready made family? But Mick bull headedly had plunged on with his plans. Five years later, in 1928, just before Mick and Madge's fourth child was born, they had returned to Indiana from Ohio and rented a house in Converse, Indiana. Mick had found a job as a farm hand nearby. Two years later, when that job petered out, he signed on with the Malleable Iron Works in Marion, where some of the family was already working. He arranged to stay with Pete and sent money home to Madge, who was never very good with money.

Many nights after boarders and husband and children were in bed, Pete and Mick would stay up talking. Things had never been good between Mick and Madge; and now they were worse. Madge was unstable, as unstable as the nation. Both Pete and Mick were worried about the kids, and in addition to Mick and Madge's four, there were

Madge's three daughters from her first marriage. Madge's family, who lived nearby, might help with the first set of children, but they had made it clear that they wouldn't help with the Detamore set.

In October of that same year, the town marshal of Converse sent Mick a note, which said, "Your wife is about to lose her house and be set out on the street. If you want your children, come and get them. I won't interfere."

That night after supper, the note was brought out and Pete and Mick and Pete's husband, Bob Holcomb, with Roy and Bob and a good friend and fellow boarder, Duckie Frill, all sat around the large round table in the kitchen and discussed the situation. Pete and her husband agreed to help with the kids. Duckie Frill volunteered his car to go get the kids and Roy and Bob thought they should go along.

It was only a few miles from Marion to Converse, but in 1930 the roads weren't good. On a clear day with the leaves turning gold and orange and crimson, Mick, Roy, Bob and Duckie loaded themselves into Duckie's car and chugged up to Converse.

Mick had been worried about what Madge would do, but she must have been overwhelmed by four stout fellows barging into her house. She also knew she soon would have no place to go and no place to take her babies. Mick simply said to her, "Madge, I am taking the kids. I know you are being put out and you have no place to go." Madge had just stared into space seeing nothing.

Roy and Bob stuffed a few ragged clothes into bags. Ducky Frill picked up the blond, plump baby, Phillip, and took three year old Nora by the hand and headed for the car saying, "You wanna ride in the ole motor car?" Ducky was an unusually handsome young man and that day he was on a mission.

Mick had spoken to his oldest sons, "Bill and Wendell, you are coming with me." They cast a worried look backwards as he ushered them out to the car. As they hurried to the car, nine year old Martha ran after Mick. She pulled at his sleeve and begged, "Mick, please take me with you. You're the only daddy I've ever known." Mick had looked down at her tenderly but had to say, "Martha, Honey, I am sorry. I love you, but I've got all I can do to take care of my own." There had been tears in his eyes as he turned away from her sobbing form. She was the youngest of his stepdaughters and his favorite.

So in 1930, the four little faces had first come to Bucktown, a section of Marion, Indiana. It was then a rough neighborhood of working class poor with its shabby, unpainted houses surrounding the belching, smelly Malleable Iron Works, which stretched a full block wide and two blocks long. Pete's husband worked there as well as Roy and Mick. She had a couple other boarders who worked there and an even greater number of the ironworkers ate lunch at the boarding house. The house was on Miller Avenue facing one of the giant sides of the Malleable.

Running a boarding house was a great deal of work. So was helping with Mick's children and caring for her own family. It all became too much. Her health suffered. After a year, they all sat down again and discussed options. That was when Mick tried to make a sensible decision and placed the children in the nearby orphans' home, the Marion Children's Home. It was November of 1931. His heart was breaking, but he couldn't work and take care of four little kids, and he couldn't afford a housekeeper. There were few childcare facilities available at this time in history.

The Orphans Home

Nora remembered a man coming to her Aunt Pete's and talking to them. He said he was going to take them for a ride. She didn't understand what was happening but she took Phillip by the hand, and said, "Let's go ride in the car." And that is what they did.

The home was not a bad experience for any of the four, but it was not home. Many times there were visitors. When they had been there almost nine months, the administration contacted Mick, and sought his permission for Nora to be adopted. There was a couple interested in taking her for their own. They encouraged him to give his consent for the adoption of all four.

Mick was 33 years old, with little education and a job that was not very dependable. He had little to offer the four children he had help bring into the world. But he was their father, and in his own way, he knew he could not let them be separated. What was he going to do? Pete had tried and it had been too much. He then motored to Converse and sat down and talked to Forrest and Rosie, his older brother and wife. Rosie agreed to try helping with the kids, but Rosie had three of her own, and two with special needs. So even though Mick removed his children from the Orphans' Home, he was not sure Rosie could handle the seven of them together. But it would give him a little time to think of what else he could do. He felt desperate. Even if his children would be better off with adoptive families, Mick could not bear the thought of it. Family is family, and you keep your children even if all you have to offer is your poverty and your pride.

As Mick feared, the time with Rosie was short, just a matter of weeks. Rosie was a nervous woman anyway, and she just couldn't handle that many children. Her Kenneth had poor vision and Dado could not talk plainly. She felt herself becoming resentful that her own children had problems and Mick's four were so healthy. So Mick was back to Square One. That was when he came up with the sneak/split plan, two little faces to Pete's and two to Mary's. Maybe if he just dropped them off at Pete's and Mary's, they would keep them for awhile until he could come up with another plan.

And that is what happened. He packed up his four children and carried them and their pitiful little boxes of clothes and dumped them on Pete and Mary's porches, back to Bucktown. Then he stayed away a few days, so that Pete and Mary would get over their first rush of anger and dismay at his actions and would begin to understand that he did the only thing he knew to do. The four little faces belonged to this family and he had to keep them. They were his life; they were all he had.

Poverty and Pride

Poverty and Pride
It's all I have ever known
I've lived it
And I will die with it.
But a man must have something
To hold himself together.
SO I'll hold onto my pride
And hold onto my children
And what they become
God only knows.
But they will always have each other.

Pete's Promise

Pete roused herself. She had fallen asleep in the rocker. She sensed peace surround her, a calm and peace that she had not had for a long time. What had she been doing? Oh, yes, she had been sorting out the stories concerning the four little faces. And she had begun to pray for wisdom and strength. Then she had fallen asleep. She remembered her mother saying often to her children, "Go to sleep. God is awake."

Yes, God was awake. The lives of these four little faces did not depend entirely on her strength. Her strength was in her God and she was reminded of His great love for all of us. Yes, perhaps, Mick had made some poor choices, but no child is a mistake. And the God she had given her heart to was a God of love and He loved Bill, and Wendell and Nora and Phillip. They were first of all His four little faces. He had a plan for them, a plan to give them a hope and a future. And she was part of that plan. She would help Mick with his children as much as she could, and if she got no thanks, maybe her reward would be four young lives a little happier, a little more secure, and a little healthier than if she were not part of their lives. Even in these Depression years, with God's help, she would find a way to help feed them, and find a way to keep them in school. She had spent her 37 years raising children, first her mother's; then her own, and now her nieces and nephews. There would be a way. Investing her life in children would be her life.

The year was 1932. It was late summer. Pete got up from the rocking chair, stretched and went to bed. God was awake.

How Imperfect

How imperfect are our prayers,
But He who was in on creation's plan
And knows how limited is finite man,
Comes to us,
And interprets our prayers
And translates them to the Father's heart.

Pictures

Four Little Faces

Here with Aunt Pete

The Three Story Tellers

Nora as a child

Nora as a young teen
On the farm

Nora on the farm
With Mick and Rags

Nora and Loralyn
The young mother

Nora with hubby, Wilbur and children, Danny and Loralyn

Nora and six of her siblings

Three of the faces in Uniform

The Four Faces, their last picture together

The Four Faces and Lenora with Aunt Mary's and Tressie's Kids

Madge Belle Highley
Mother of the Four Little Faces
A collage of her family including her mother, Ida
Culp and Ida's parents, Lewis and Harriet Mcbee
Culp, with Ida and husband, Leroy Hghley

Madge with son, Highley, daughter, Lillian and Madge's
two sisters, Hattie and Clove and a few grandchildren.

Leroy Highley

Mick Detamore and Siblings

Reunion with siblings

His Brothers and sisters
Fern, Roy, Dona, Mary, Ivan, Pery
Forrest, viole (Bud); Cecil (Pete)

The Nine

Deloss Detamore and three of his sons including Mick

Eli Detamore, Mick's grandfather

Nora Rust Detamore, Mick's mother and her sisters

John Rust

John Rust, Nora's father

Mick at the fair
With Loralyn and Danny
(1956)

The Farmhouse in Jennings County

Collages of Detamore Aunts and Uncles
With some spouses and children

John & Elma Rust

Nora Rust Dotamore (our great grandmother) Born Feb 1872 died in 1915 with Uncle Bob's birth ✝ 9-5-1891

Aunt Cecil Born 1895 More with James

Iuon (&) George Graham

Georgiane & M. Billy 3 children; also Glen, Doris John (&) with & Katy wife Pat & sons

Glen George and Graham

Iuon born 1900

Daughter Lerue & Penny Bird Daughter Charlene Jim also Tom born later

Pete was (&) to Bob Holcomb Son James Killed in WWII African Invasion

Forrest born 1892

Sons: Kenneth, Harry & Dude. Only Harry married

Forrest (Pets) with wife Doris

Fern born 1911 with daughter Judy Fern was (&) to George Hedges 1 son who died from Rabies as a child

Harry's Children: Harry, David, Leroy, Floyd Rose, Amanda, Vernice

Bobby Bennett

Leona Bennett Wyne
with husband & son
Raymond, also had
daughter, Nora
(This is Aunt Tressie's
children. Son Bobby had
3 sons, David, Wayne?)
Tressie was born 1896.

Roy
(born
1910)
here
with
wife
Marie
They had four sons: Ronnie
Paula
Kirk

End of pictures

The Growing Up Years

The Great Depression stretched on through the 30s. It was not an easy time to grow up. Sometimes Mick and the four little faces would live with Pete; once Mary and her husband, Ed, and their growing brood of children lived with Mick and the four little faces in a house Mick had rented. At times Mick would rent a house and another of his siblings would live with them and be the house keeper. At least two did; one was Fern and the other was Bud who was really Volney. Uncle Bud never married and was a veteran of WWI, drew a pension. He taught the kids how to play Euchre and how to shuffle a mean deck of cards. Sometimes, Mick was able to hire a housekeeper for a short time, but overall, housekeepers didn't last long, and as the children got older, they pretty much took care of themselves and each other. Bill became the shopper, and the meal planner and the cook. One winter he got sick and after missing so much school, just dropped out, and took a job. With things so tight much of that time, a little extra money went a long way. Phillip would do the same thing a few years later. Now Nora loved school but could not learn to read. We believe she had a learning disability called dyslexia. (She only started reading after her 18th birthday.) So she also dropped out of school at about 16. Only Wendell finished high school. He was also on the basketball team.

The years of the Depression meant hunger for some people, but the Detamore children did not remember being hungry. They ate a lot of beans though. Before school, they would take the pan with beans soaking to Aunt Mary's house. She would cook them all morning.

Then when the children were out of school for lunch, they would take the beans home, eating them with light bread. It took two of the children to carry the beans, a handle for each. They would have the beans for supper with fried potatoes. This was the meal they had sometimes seven days a week. Candy was a very rare treat, and so were any sweets. There was not much meat. The fruit eaten was usually stewed dried prunes, peaches or apricots. In the summer, sometimes, there was a small garden. Coupons were used for meat and sugar. Coupons were also used for shoes. New clothes were rare. Hand me downs were the rule of the day. A story is told that Phillip got his nick name, 'Rags' from a neighbor, who laughingly but not unkindly, observed the small boy one day, and said to him, "Ah, here comes the raggedy man". The name stuck.

Growing up during the Depression also meant some people did unusual things in order to provide food for their children. One of the neighbors plowed his garden with his wife harnessed to the garden plow. It was both a sad and funny thing to see.

Then just when Wendell and William were old enough to be soldiers, the country became involved in WWII. So they both went overseas. So did Jamie. Jamie was Aunt Pete's only son. Phillip went into the service at eighteen and after the war ended. All of Mick's boys came home without a scratch. Jamie was killed on a beach landing. It was not only a sad day for Aunt Pete and Lenora when they were notified of his death, but a sad day for the whole family. He is buried at Peru. He was one of those boys who loved his family and his country and would have made a fine neighbor.

Sadly, the war brought an end to the Great Depression. It was good to be out of an economic depression. It was bad to be involved in a war.

Wendell married when he went into the military and had fathered a son, also named Wendell. When he and Bill returned in 1946 they both gave Mick a granddaughter, Bernice, and Billie. Months later in

1947, Nora added another granddaughter whose name did not start with a B but an L.

In the years Bill and Wendell were in the military, they sent money home to Mick. They thought of it as their money. Mick thought of it as his. So he used the money to fulfill one of his dreams. He bought a farm in Jennings County, near his sisters, Ivan and Dona, who had married Jennings County men when their father, Deloss Detamore, had taken his family to Jennings for four years. Those were the years 1915-1920, the years following the death of his wife, Nora Rust. At that time, the farm was near Graham Church. Ivan lived near Graham Church as well.

The farm Mick bought was in Lovett Township. The year was 1945. It was just before the end of the war. Mick had been a good farmhand in his younger days but he had forgotten how hard the work was and how demanding it was. He had brought Nora and Phillip with him, and they were not happy with life in Jennings County. After a year, they went back to Marion. That is when Phillip signed up for military duty and Nora went to work in a shoe factory. As usual she dated often and had two or three offers of marriage, but turned down her suitors. She ended up returning to Jennings County and marrying one of the men she had dated there, a neighbor who farmed for someone else, Wilbur Reynolds. She and Wilbur added a son, Danny, in 1948, a little brother to their daughter, Loralyn, her own living doll. At 18 months older, she took her sisterly responsibilities seriously.

Bill and Wendell remained in Marion and raised families. Phillip came home to Marion in 1952 and married Betty Betts in 1953. They added two more granddaughters to Mick's burgeoning family, Debra and Phyllis. In all, Bill, who had married Eunice Mc Carty in February of 1946, had three daughters, Billie, Rebecca, and Jackie. Wendell, married to childhood sweetheart, Mary Ethel Renn, ended up with four living children, Wendell, Niece, Marilyn and Rick.

A Funny Story

It must have been Uncle Rags (Phillip) who told this story when we were all talking about the move to Jennings County. It sounded so much like my grandfather that I knew most of it had to be true.

Mick, and Phillip and Nora finally left Marion in May of 1945. They were loaded up the month before. The ancient truck, a 1931 black Chevy, one and a half ton truck made it to Alexandria before they threw a rod. They limped back to Marion to the Ninth Street House they had just vacated. Across the street lived a good mechanic. His name was Biscuit Bryant. (that was what Uncle Rags said).

Mick talked Biscuit into working on the motor, with Phillip doing the work and Biscuit telling him what to do. Then after they were finished, Mick insisted on tightening-tightening too much and the work had to be redone. Biscuit gave Mick a hearty cussing out and added, "I told the boy what to do and he did what I told him to do."

Finally, the Farm

Finally, on the second day of May, Dick Jordan, a son-in-law to Aunt Donie, came up from Jennings County and took down a load of horses followed by Phillip and Nora in a Model A Ford, and Mick in the repaired truck loaded with farm machinery and household goods. They spent the night with Donie whose house was in Lovett, and left in a hurry the next morning, being chased out of the house by cussing Dr. John Green, the colorful country doctor who had been called to attend the birth of Donie's fourth child, Dean Hoffman. Donie was forty years old with three grown children, but she enjoyed this child as she had not been able to enjoy the others. It is often the way with mid life babies.

They were late getting a crop in that year, but not too late. Besides farming, the men of the county were required to work on the road for so many days. That is how Mick and Phillip met Wilbur. They were part of the same road crew. Then they introduced him to Nora.

When Nora came back to Jennings in 1947 to marry Wilbur, they agreed to live with her dad. That did not last a long time, because the two men were too much alike, stubborn and bull headed, but it was a good arrangement for a short time.

Shortly before Loralyn's birth, Nora went to throw out the dishwater, and noticed one of the mules had gotten tangled and was pulling and tugging at his entrapments. It was only mid-morning and neither Wilbur nor Mick were expected home for hours. Wilbur was at his job at the Robbins Sawmill and Mick was working on the road that day for the county. Nora continued to watch and her tender heart finally could stand it no more. She waddled out to detangle the mule and succeeded somewhat in freeing the mule but got herself entangled, and the mule dragged her several yards on her very round tummy before the mule was separated from his deliverer. Nora was breathless, and trembling, and it was some time before she could stand upright and return to the house. It seemed funny to her later but not to Mick and Wilbur when she chuckled with the retelling at supper. Neither she nor the baby were harmed.

On her due date, Nora fixed a large Sunday dinner with fried chicken, and called in the men. Mick was ploughing through his dinner in his typical fashion when he looked up from his plate and said to Nora, "What is wrong?" She began to describe her back ache, rubbing her back as she did so, and added how she had been feeling all morning. Mick pushed back the plate of his unfinished dinner, got up from the table, exclaiming, "Girl, you're going to have a baby, and I mean today." He was out of the door to bring the car around, food forgotten.

By the time Loralyn was born, Pete had loaded up her family which included her daughter, Lenora and Lenora's husband, Reed Bird, and three of Lenora's children, Doralee, Jim (named after his uncle Jamie) and Charles. She brought them to a farm she had bought near Mick's farm. So after a time in the hospital Nora and Loralyn went to Pete's and Pete asked to name the baby girl in exchange for her care of Nora and the baby. She chose the name Lora because it rhymed with Nora and Dora and Lenora and was easy for Nora to spell. She also put only one 'n' on the Lyn, again easier for Nora.

Nora and the baby went back to Mick's after a few weeks, but came back in October of 1948. Danny was born the first day of the month at Aunt Pete's and Dr. Matthews was paid $35.00 in dimes for his services. Wilbur had saved the dimes for such a time.

Most family holiday dinners were spent at Aunt Pete's. There were also family gatherings at Aunt Donie's and Aunt Ivan's. And sometimes in October, a family gathering would occur at Wilbur and Nora's in honor of Danny's birthday. For this gathering, cream was kept back and homemade ice cream was the treat of the day. The meal was always pitch-in. All the aunts were great cooks. Conversation and food flowed.

Usually the group included only the Jennings County Detamores but sometimes Aunt Mary and some of her family would come and sometimes Bill's family or Rags' family. Often, Aunt Fern came from Indianapolis with her family.

Pete and her family stayed on the farm for several years, then sold the place and bought a house near Donie in Lovett. They later built a house in the same little town. It was called 'The Bird House'.

The Grown Four Little Faces

As adults, and after their military service, William, 'Bill'; Wendell, 'Lefty' and Phillip, 'Rags' settled into jobs in Marion. Bill became a skilled latherer and the boy who was clumsy became a man that climbed ladders and scaffolding daily. Lefty joined his father-law and brother-in-law in their family- run roofing business. Rags chose factory work or maybe the work chose him. Marion, at that time, was largely an automobile parts city like Kokomo and New Castle. It was a factory town.

Nora stayed home with her children until they were in school. Then she began working here and there part time for neighbors. Eventually, she began nursing jobs, nursing older folks whose families were worn out from years of caretaking and needed something of a break. After a few years of that, she went to work at Regal Rugs and retired from there. She was a trimmer. Her favorite job was the nursing but those jobs were emotional exhausting.

All the four little faces were responsible parents, raising children that had a strong work ethic and faith in family. Several of the children went to college. In the wonder of God's planning, all the wives of the three male little faces were or became Christian women early in their marriages. Bill, Lefty and Rags took a little longer to take hold of faith in God, but they were good men and wonderful uncles. They helped Wilbur finish his house in the sixties, and visited Nora and her family once or twice a year. Nora and Wilbur and their kids would try every year to attend the Detamore Reunion in Marion the third weekend of

August. The Detamores had been meeting since 1905. The last large reunion was in 2002 and was unofficial. It was at Rags' funeral. The man who worked so hard to keep the reunion going finally got his wish, a large contingent of Detamores gathered to honor a well loved relative and friend. He was a man who loved well.

Personal Note: If you are reading this now, and you knew these men, you may be raising your eyebrows and saying to yourself, "Obviously, the writer didn't know these men very well. She is ignoring their glaring faults."

And the response to this is, "Yes, I did see their glaring faults just as I saw my grandfather's and just as I see my own and others, but their love for me and my love for them far outweighed their faults. What else can I say??" I guess I could quote scripture but it says almost the same thing: "Love covers a multitude of sins"." (I Peter 4:8)

On Life's Pages

You are the same throuout the ages
You have helped me turn life's pages
You've been there when the storm rages
And you've delivered me from the cages
Of selfishness and transgressions
And Jesus paid the wages
For my sins!

Yes, You've been there through all the stages
Of my life
And You've been there
When the sages commune with me
And I feel your presence.
Almighty God, you are to me!

Almighty God, you are to me.
Helping me turn life's pages
Until we meet face to face,
And your image is imprinted
Fully, on my final stage.
Lord, I long for that day!

Mick, the Boy, Mick the Man

This story is about my mother and her three brothers, but it is also about my grandfather, Percy Odwick Detamore. He left a legacy that cannot be denied. He did keep his children together, and for that I am thankful. He had a tough/tender character and was a bundle of contradictions. There is no question of his love for them. Yet, he could be abusive, especially verbally. He sometimes seemed to put his lady friend above his kids. I do not condemn him. Raising four children by oneself was no picnic.

The grandchildren all looked at him a little differently. Some of them see him as just 'Mick', the man they knew as their grandfather and had to endure once in awhile. For some he was Grandpa, a man they were mildly fond of because he was their Father's father. For my brother and I, he was truly all he was born to be, a loving and tender grandfather, who played with us, believed in us, and showed up for the important happenings in our lives. One of my fondest memories is standing on his feet at the county fair, so I could look through the fence at the racing horses. He and I were always close, from the time of my birth to the end. He died when I was in Europe in 1981, but he was on my mind. I am sorry I was not there to help and hold his hand. I loved him, even though I could see his poor decisions and the consequences they brought. He told me he never loved my grandmother. I think that was sad for both of them. She was mentally ill, not a bad person, just one with an illness that we still know very little of. He never remarried. He was respected by his sons because 'he taught them how to work', and for all of them that was a redeeming quality. It was who they were, good workers who provided for their families and kept them together, just as Mick had done for them. And they looked out for each other, all their lives.

I was always trying to talk him into a good story, and once asked how he got his nickname. The following is my version of that story. In my own way, I see that naming story as a pivotal point in his life. You make your own decision. But remember that the boy is the father of the man.

The Naming

The mules plodded along the hard packed dirt of the country road. The tousled headed boy of eleven opened one eye and reached for the edge of the wagon. He pulled himself up and glanced at the awakening sky. Straight in front of him was an enormous orange ball filling the eastern horizon. It rather startled him. In minutes, the ball was gone and the sky was diffused with light.

It was a lovely midsummer morning, hot as Indiana should be at that time of year, 1910.

They were to see Ben Agnes that morning, the man who owned the land they farmed. The boy had never met him. This farm was near Converse, Indiana.

His dad was going to buy a milk cow. There was another new baby at home and his mother was expecting again, so she needed the cow.

Deloss Detamore had four sons, and three worked the farm right alongside him including the boy, who now glanced over at his older brother, Forrest. Forrest was known as Fats, but the once fat little boy had become a well-muscled young man of eighteen. This early rising when it was still dark was nothing new to them. They were usually up at this time helping with milking and feeding. The boy was big for his age and strong, with the promise of being a fine-looking man. His many sisters and brothers were fond of him. He was a mixture of teasing boy and tender brother. With a theatrical flare, his gentle mother, Nora Rust, had given most of her children a name starting with 'O'. He did not know why. His name was Percy Odwick. He did not like his name and even envied Forrest his unbecoming nickname.

The wagon turned into a long lane leading to a large white farmhouse with many out buildings. The wagon moved around the house and toward the barn. There Ben Agnes waited, a big florid man with reddish hair turning gray. He gave a hearty greeting to the boys' pa, and Deloss returned the greeting, stopped the team and told Forrest to hold the team. The boy climbed down from the wagon.

"Well, well, well," Ben Agnes boomed, "I have not met this one. What is his name?"

To the boy's surprise, his father looked over at him with a grin, and stated, "This one is Mick," and the name stuck.

For Mick, the day could not have been grander. To be renamed by his father seemed like a special benediction. Deloss Detamore was not easy on his sons. He expected lots of work from them and praise was infrequent and moments of closeness rare. Being big for his age, and one of the older children, Mick was often referred to as the work mule of the family, sometimes in jest and sometimes sadly. But work he knew how to do and it became his lifeline, as a boy and as a man.

Holiday Dinners

(A note from the author)

Like my mother, I looked forward to Holiday dinners. When I was big enough, I got to help. I remember helping Doralee wash the celery and then sometimes we got to help cut up fruit for the special holiday fruit salad. Both the fruit salad and the bean salad were traditional favorites and Aunt Pete's recipes. Let me share them with you.

Holiday Fruit Salad

Two oranges, and two apples, one red and one yellow, cut into chunks. Add a can of sliced peaches, cut up and a can of crushed pineapple. Then a can of cherries or a bottle of cherries. Add a couple tablespoons of sugar and a little juice from the peaches. Drink the rest. Add red grapes and nuts if desired. Just before serving, add two sliced bananas.

Bean Salad

Two cans fancy red kidney beans, drained and rinsed. To the beans, add one small onion, chopped, and celery, if desired. Add chopped sweet pickle to taste. Then add two chopped hard boiled eggs. Add a dressing made of a cup of salad dressing, a small amount of sugar and a bit of the pickle juice.

When you have enjoyed your holiday dinner, play a game of euchre with old friends and family members you lost to last year. When I was a child, I could not wait to get big enough to play euchre. I must never have grown up. I don't remember ever getting to play. We took walks when we got too old for games with the boys, and I learned a lot on those walks.

Holidays are for times for families to share, laugh and hug, and to remember how much we mean to each other. Especially because we have shared some of each others' sorrows as well as their joys. That is what families are for. That is what my family knows, because that is what my family has always done.

Printed in the United States
By Bookmasters